ALL

the collected

short poems

1923 - 1958

Books by Louis Zukofsky

An "Objectivists" Anthology
Le Style Apollinaire
First Half or "A"— 9
55 Poems
Anew
A Test of Poetry
A Test of Poetry (English edition)
Some Time
Barely and widely
5 Statements for Poetry
"A" 1–12
It was
16 once published
I's (pronounced *eyes*)
Bottom: on Shakespeare
Found Objects

ALL

the collected

short poems

1923 - 1958

Louis Zukofsky

 W · W · NORTON & COMPANY · INC · New York

Library of Congress Catalog Card No. 65-11001

Published simultaneously in the Dominion of
Canada by George J. McLeod Limited, Toronto

Printed in the United States of America
for the Publishers by the Vail-Ballou Press, Inc.

1 2 3 4 5 6 7 8 9 0

ALL
the collected short poems 1923–1958

to
Paul

Contents

55 Poems

اسرار جهان چنانکه در دفتر ماست

گفتن نتوان که آن وبال سر ماست

چون نیست درین مردم دانا اهلی

نتوان گفتن هرآنچه در خاطر ماست

عمر خیام

Poem beginning "The"

Because I have had occasion to remember, quote, paraphrase, I dedicate this poem to Anyone and Anything I have unjustifiably forgotten. Also to J. S. Bach—309,* Bede's *Ecclesiastical History* —248, 291, Max Beerbohm—245, Beethoven's *Ninth Symphony*— 310–312, Broadway—134, Geoffrey Chaucer—1st Movement, Title, College Cheer—45, E. E. Cummings' *Is Five*—38, Dante— 66, Norman Douglas' *South Wind*—14, Elijah, the Prophet—24, T. S. Eliot's *The Waste Land* and *The Sacred Wood*—25–27, John Erskine—184, 185, Heinrich Heine—266, 267, 269, 316, Robert Herrick—187, 188, Horace—141, Horses—224–237, Aldous Huxley's *Those Barren Leaves*—12, 18, Henry James— 2nd Movement, Title, Jewish Folk Song—191, 270–280, James Joyce—13, 20, 28, 29, D. H. Lawrence—8, 19, 133, Christopher Marlowe's *Edward II*—46, 47, Modern Advertising—163, George Moore—24, Marianne Moore—22, Mussolini—74, 75, Myself— 130, 142, 167, 309, Obvious—Where the Reference is Obvious, Walter Pater's *Renaissance*—165, *Peer Gynt*—281–285, Poe's *Helen*—168–182, Popular Non-Sacred Song—4, 5, 36, 37, 288, 289, Ezra Pound—15, 18, Power of the Past, Present, and Future— Where the reference is to the word Sun, E. A. Robinson's *Children of the Night*—132, Sophocles—6, Oswald Spengler—132, Max Stirner—199–202, Symbol of our Relatively Most Permanent Self, Origin and Destiny—Wherever the reference is to the word Mother, *The Bible*—1–3, 9, 313, 314, The Bolsheviki—203, 323, The French Language—31, 33, 51, 292, The King's English—166, *The Merchant of Venice*—250–265, The Yellow Menace—241– 242, University Extension—70, Villon—21, Franz Werfel—68, Virginia Woolf's *Mrs. Dalloway*—52, Yehoash—110–129, 205– 223, 318–330.

* References following dashes are to lines in *Poem beginning "The."*

11

Poem beginning "The"

1 The
2 Voice of Jesus I. Rush singing
3   in the wilderness
4 A boy's best friend is his mother,
5 It's your mother all the time.
6 Residue of Oedipus-faced wrecks
7 Creating out of the dead,—
8 From the candle flames of the souls of dead mothers
9 Vide the legend of thin Christ sending her
          out of the temple,—
10 Books from the stony heart, flames rapping
          the stone,
11 Residue of self-exiled men
12 By the Tyrrhenian.
13   Paris.
14 But everywhere only the South Wind, the
          sirocco, the broken Earth-face.
15 The broken Earth-face, the age demands an
          image of its life and contacts,
16 Lord, lord, not that we pray, are sure of
          the question,
17 But why are our finest always dead?
18 And why, Lord, this time, is it Mauberly's
          Luini in porcelain, why is it Chelifer,
19 Why is it Lovat who killed Kangaroo,
20 Why Stephen Daedalus with the cane of
          ash,
21 But why les neiges?
22 And why, if all of Mary's Observations
          have been made
23 Have not the lambs become more sapient
          drinking of the spring;
24 Kerith is long dry, and the ravens that

brought the prophet bread
25 Are dust in the waste land of a raven-
       winged evening.
26 And why if the waste land has been explored,
       traveled over, circumscribed,
27 Are there only wrathless skeletons exhumed
       new planted in its sacred wood,
28 Why—heir, long dead,—Odysseus, wandering of ten years
29 Out-journeyed only by our Stephen, bibbing
       of a day,
30 O why is that to Hecuba as Hecuba to he!
31 You are cra-a-zee on the subject of babies,
       says she,
32 That is because somehow our authors have been
       given a woman's intuition.
33 Il y a un peu trop de femme in this South Wind.
34 And on the cobblestones, bang, bang, bang,
       myself like the wheels—
35 The tram passes singing
36 O do you take this life as your lawful wife,
37   I do!
38 O the Time is 5
39   I do!
40 O the Time is 5
41   I do!
42 O do you take these friends as your loves
       to wive,
43 O the Time is 5
44   I do!

45 For it's the hoo-doos, the somethin' voo-doos
46 And not Kings onelie, but the wisest men
47 Graue Socrates, what says Marlowe?
48 For it was myself seemed held
49 Beating—beating—
50 Body trembling as over an hors d'oeuvres—
51
52 And the dream ending—Dalloway! Dalloway—
53 The blind portals opening, and I awoke!

54 Let me be
55 Not by art have we lived,

56 Not by graven images forbidden to us
57 Not by letters I fancy,
58 Do we dare say
59 With Spinoza grinding lenses, Rabbaisi,
60 After living on Cathedral Parkway?

SECOND MOVEMENT: *International Episode*

61 This is the aftermath
62 When Peter Out and I discuss the theatre.
63 Evenings, our constitutional.
64 We both strike matches, both in unison,
65   to light one pipe, my own.
66 'Tis, 'tis love, that makes the world go
        round and love is what I dream.
67 Peter is polite and I to me am almost as
        polite as Peter.
68 Somehow, in Germany, the Jew goat-song
        is unconvincing—
69   How the brain forms its visions think-
        ing incessantly of the things,
70 Not the old Greeks anymore,—
71   the things themselves a shadow world
        scarce shifting the incessant
        thought—
72 Time, time the goat were an offering,
73 Eh, what show do we see tonight, Peter?
74 "Il Duce: I feel God deeply."
75   Black shirts—black shirts—some power
        is so funereal.

76 Lion-heart, frate mio, and so on in two
        languages
77 the thing itself a shadow world.
78 Goldenrod
79 Of which he is a part,
80 Sod
81 He hurried over
82 Underfoot,
83 Make now
84 His testament of sun and sky
85 With clod

14

86　To root what shoot
87　It sends to run the sun,
88　The sun-sky blood.
89　My loves there is his mystery beyond
　　　　　your loves.
90　Uncanny are the stars,
91　His slimness was as evasive
92　And his grimness was not yours,

93　Do you walk slowly the halls of the heavens,
94　Or saying that you do, lion-hearted not ours,
95　Hours, days, months, past from us and gone,
96　Lion-heart not looked upon, walk with the
　　　　　stars.
97　Or have these like old men acknowledged
98　No kin but that grips of death,
99　Of being dying only to live on with them
100　Entirely theirs,
101　And so quickly grown old that we on earth like
　　　　　stems raised dark
102　Feel only the lull, heave, phosphor
　　　　　change, death, the
103　One follow, the other, the end?

104　Our candles have been buried beneath these
　　　　　waters,
105　Their lights are his,
106　Ship-houses on the waters he might have lived
　　　　　near.
107　Steady the red light and it makes no noise
　　　　　whatever.
108　Damn it! they have made capital of his flesh
　　　　　and bone.
109　What, in revenge, can dead flesh and bone
　　　　　make capital?
110　And his heart is dry
111　Like the teeth of a dead camel
112　But his eyes no longer blink
113　Not even as a blind dog's.

114　With the blue night shadows on the sand
115　May his kingdom return to him,

15

116 The Bedouin leap again on his *asilah*,
117 The expanse of heaven hang upon his shoulder
118 As an embroidered texture,
119 Behind him on his saddle sit the night
120 Sing into his ear:

121 Swifter than a tiger to his prey,
122 Lighter than the storm wind, dust or spray,
123 The Bedouin bears the Desert-Night,
124 Big his heart and young with life,
125 Younger yet his gay, wild wife
126   The Desert-Night.

127 Some new trappings for his steed,
128 All the stars in dowry his meed
129   From the Desert-Night.

130 I've changed my mind, Zukofsky,
131 How about some other show—
132 "The Queen of Roumania," "Tilbury,"
        "The West-Decline,"
133 "Hall's Mills," "The Happy Quetzal-
        coatl,"
134 "Near Ibsen," "Dancing with H. R. H.,"
        "Polly Wants a New Fur Coat,"
135 "The Post Office"—
136 Speaking of the post office, the following
        will handicap you for the position,
137   my dear Peter,
138 Your weight less than one hundred
        twenty-five pounds,
139 One half of a disabled veteran, and
        probably
140   the whole of an unknown soldier,
141 That's indomitaeque morti for you.

142 Is it true what you say, Zukofsky,
143 Sorry to say, My Peter Out.

144 "Tear the Codpiece Off, A Musical
        Comedy,"
145 Likewise, "Panting for Pants,"

16

"The Dream That Knows No Waking."

THIRD MOVEMENT: *In Cat Minor*

147 Hard, hard the cat-world.
148 On the stream Vicissitude
149 Our milk flows lewd.

150 We'll cry, we'll cry,
151 We'll cry the more
152 And wet the floor,

153 Megrow, megrow,
154 Around around,
155 The only sound

156 The prowl, our prowl,
157 Of gentlemen cats
158 With paws like spats

159 Who weep the nights
160 Till the nights are gone—
161 —And r-r-run—the Sun!

FOURTH MOVEMENT: *More "Renaissance"*

162 Is it the sun you're looking for,
163 Drop in at Askforaclassic, Inc.,
164 Get yourself another century,
165 A little frost before sundown,
166 It's the times don'chewknow,
167 And if you're a Jewish boy, then be your
     Plato's Philo.

168 Engprof, thy lectures were to me
169   Like those roast flitches of red boar
170 That, smelling, one is like to see
171   Through windows where the steam's galore
172   Like our own "Cellar Door."

173 On weary bott'm long wont to sit,
174   Thy graying hair, thy beaming eyes,

175 Thy heavy jowl would make me fit
176   For the Pater that was Greece,
177   The siesta that was Rome.

178 Lo! from my present—say not—itch
179   How statue-like I see thee stand
180 Phi Beta Key within thy hand!
181   Professor—from the backseats which
182 Are no man's land!

183 Poe,
184 Gentlemen, don'chewknow,
185 But never wrote an epic.

FIFTH MOVEMENT: *Autobiography*

186 Speaking about epics, mother,
187 How long ago is it since you gathered
        mushrooms,
188 Gathered mushrooms while you mayed.
189 It is your mate, my father, boating.
190 A stove burns like a full moon in a desert night.
191 Un in hoyze is kalt. You think of a new
        grave,
192 In the fields, flowers.
193 Night on the bladed grass, bayonets dewed.
194 It is your mate, my father, boating.
195 Speaking about epics, mother,—
196 Down here among the gastanks, ruts,
        cemetery-tenements—
197 It is your Russia that is free.
198 And I here, can I say only—
199   "So then an egoist can never embrace
            a party
200   Or take up with a party?
201   Oh, yes, only he cannot let himself
202   Be embraced or taken up by the party."
203 It is your Russia that is free, mother.
204 Tell me, mother.

205 Winged wild geese, where lies the passage,
206 In far away lands lies the passage.

207   Winged wild geese, who knows the pathway?
208   Of the winds, asking, we shall say:
209   Wind of the South and wind of the North
210   Where has our sun gone forth?
211   Naked, twisted, scraggly branches,
212   And dark, gray patches through the branches,
213   Ducks with puffed-up, fluttering feathers
214   On a cobalt stream.
215   And faded grass that's slowly swaying.
216   A barefoot shepherd boy
217   Striding in the mire:
218   Swishing indifferently a peeled branch
219   On jaded sheep.
220   An old horse strewn with yellow leaves
221   By the edge of the meadow
222   Draws weakly with humid nostrils
223   The moisture of the clouds.
224   Horses that pass through inappreciable
woodland,
225   Leaves in their manes tangled, mist, autumn
green,
226   Lord, why not give these bright brutes—
your good land—
227   Turf for their feet always, years for their mien.
228   See how each peer lifts his head, others follow,
229   Mate paired with mate, flanks coming full
they crowd,
230   Reared in your sun, Lord, escaping each hollow
231   Where life-struck we stand, utter their praise
aloud.
232   Very much Chance, Lord, as when you first
made us,
233   You might forget them, Lord, preferring what
234   Being less lovely where sadly we fuss?
235   Weed out these horses as tho they were not?
236   Never alive in brute delicate trembling
237   Song to your sun, against autumn assembling.

238   If horses could but sing Bach, mother,—
239   Remember how I wished it once—
240   Now I kiss you who could never sing Bach,
never read Shakespeare.

19

241 In Manhattan here the Chinamen are yellow
        in the face, mother,
242 Up and down, up and down our streets they
        go yellow in the face,
243 And why is it the representatives of your,
        my, race are always hankering for
        food, mother?
244 We, on the other hand, eat so little.
245 Dawn't you think Trawtsky rawthaw a
        darrling,
246 I ask our immigrant cousin querulously.
247 Naw! I think hay is awlmawst a Tchekoff.
248 But she has more color in her cheeks than
        the Angles—Angels—mother,—
249 They have enough, though. We should
        get some more color, mother.
250 If I am like them in the rest, I should
        resemble them in that, mother,
251 Assimilation is not hard,
252 And once the Faith's askew
253 I might as well look Shagetz just as much
        as Jew.
254 I'll read their Donne as mine,
255 And leopard in their spots
256 I'll do what says their Coleridge,
257 Twist red hot pokers into knots.
258 The villainy they teach me I will execute
259 And it shall go hard with them,
260 For I'll better the instruction,
261 Having learned, so to speak, in their
        colleges.
262   It is engendered in the eyes
263   With gazing fed, and fancy dies
264   In the cradle where it lies
265   In the cradle where it lies
266 I, Senora, am the Son of the Respected
        Rabbi,
267 Israel of Saragossa,
268 Not that the Rabbis give a damn,
269 Keine Kadish wird man sagen.

270 Under the cradle the white goat stands, mother,
271 What will the goat be saddled with, mother?
272   Almonds, raisins
273 What will my heart be bartering, mother,
274   Wisdom, learning.
275 Lullaby, lullaby, lullaby, lullaby.
276 These are the words of the prophet, mother,
277 Likely to save me from Tophet, mother—
278 What will my heart be burning to, mother,
279   Wisdom, learning.
280 By the cat and the well, I swear, my
      Shulamite!
281 In my faith, in my hope, and in my love.
282 I will cradle thee, I will watch thee,
283 Sleep and dream thou, dear my boy!
284   (Presses his cheek against her mouth.)
285 I must try to fare forth from here.
286 I do not forget you,
287 I am just gone out for to-night,
288 The Royal Stag is abroad,
289 I am gone out hunting,
290 The leaves have lit by the moon.
291 Even in their dirt, the Angles like Angels
      are fair,
292 Brooks Nash, for instance, faisant un petit
      bruit, mais très net,
293 Saying, He who is afraid to do that should
      be denied the privilege,
294 And where the automobile roads with the
      gasoline shine,
295 Appropriately the katydid—
296 Ka-ty did . . . . Ka-ty didn't . . . .

297 Helen Gentile,
298 And did one want me; no.
299 But wanted me to take one? yes.
300 And should I have kissed one? no.
301 That is, embraced one first
302 And holding closely one, then kissed one?
      yes.

303   Angry against things' iron I ring

304   Recalcitrant prod and kick.

305   Oh, Baedekera Schönberg, you here

306   dreaming of the relentlessness of motion

307   As usual,

308   One or two dead in the process what does it
          matter.

309   Our God immortal such Life as is our God,

310   Bei dein Zauber, by thy magic I embrace
          thee,

311   Open Sesame, Ali Baba, I, thy firefly, little
          errant star, call here,

312   By thy magic I embrace thee.

313   O my son Sun, my son, my son Sun!
          would God

314   I had died for thee, O Sun, my son, my
          son!

315   I have not forgotten you, mother,—

316   It is a lie—Aus meinen grossen leiden mach ich
          die kleinen lieder,

317   Rather they are joy, against nothingness joy—

318   By the wrack we shall sing our Sun-song

319   Under our feet will crawl

320   The shadows of dead worlds,

321   We shall open our arms wide,

322   Call out of pure might—

323   Sun, you great Sun, our Comrade,

324   From eternity to eternity we remain true to you,

325   A myriad years we have been,

326   Myriad upon myriad shall be.

327   How wide our arms are,

328   How strong,

329   A myriad years we have been,

330   Myriad upon myriad shall be.

29 POEMS

1

Memory of V. I. Ulianov

Immemorial,
And after us
Immemorial,
O white
O orbit-trembling,
Star, thru all the leaves
Of elm;—
Lighted-one, beyond the trunk tip
Of the elm
High, proportionately vast,
Of mist and form;—
Star, of all live processes
Continual it seems to us,
Like elm leaves,
Lighted in your glow;—
We thrive in strange hegira
Here below,
Yet sometimes in our flight alone
We speak to you,
When nothing that was ours seems spent
And life consuming us seems permanent,
And flight of stirring beating up the night
And down and up; we do not sink with every wave.
Travels our consciousness
Deep in its egress.
Eclipsed the earth, for earth is power
And we of earth.
Eclipsed our death, for death is power
And we of death.
Single we are, tho others still may be with us
And we for others.
We have come to the sources of being,

Inviolable, throngs everlasting, rising forever,
Rush as of river courses,
Change within change of forces.
Irrevocable yet safe we go,
Irrevocable you, too,
O star, we speaking to you,
The shadows of the elm leaves faded,
Only the trunk of elm now dark and high
Unto your height:
Now and again you fall,
Blow dark and burn again,
And we in turn
Share now your fate
Whose process is continual.

2

Not much more than being,
Thoughts of isolate, beautiful
Being at evening, to expect
                    at a river-front:

A shaft dims
With a turning wheel;

Men work on a jetty
By a broken wagon;

Leopard, glowing-spotted,
        The summer river—
Under: The Dragon:

Cocktails
and signs of
"ads"

flashing,
light's waterfalls,

Bacchae
among electric lights

will swarm the crowds
streamers of the lighted

skyscrapers

nor tripping
over underbrush

but upon pavement

and not with thyrsus
shall they prick

the body of their loves
but waist to waist

laugh out in gyre—
announced then upon stairs,

not upon hills,
will be their flight

when passed turnstiles,
having dropped

coins
they've sprinted up

where on the air (elevated)
waves flash—and out—

leap
signaling—lights below

4

Buoy—no, how,
It is not a question: what
Is this freighter carrying?—
Did smoke blow?—That whistle?—
Of course, commerce will not complete
Anything, yet the harbor traffic is busy,
                    there shall be a complete fragment

Of—

Nothing, look! that gull
Streak the water!
Getting nearer are we,
Hear? count the dissonances,

Shoal? accost—cost
Cost accounting.

5

Ferry

Gleams, a green lamp
In the fog:
Murmur, in almost
A dialogue

Siren and signal
Siren to signal.

Parts the shore from the fog,
Rise there, tower on tower,
Signs of stray light
And of power.

Siren to signal
Siren to signal.

Hour-gongs and the green
Of the lamp.

Plash. Night. Plash. Sky.

27

6

How many
Times round

Deck, ladies?

What says
The nigger?

"Fi' minutes
After a

Man's breath
Leaves

His body
He knows—'

Much 'bout
Himself 's

Ten years
Befo' 'e

Was bo'n—"

What you
Say to

That, ladies?

The Statue
Of Liberty's

Drunk?!
French! !

7

During the Passaic Strike of 1926

the sexton of the rich parish of St. Mark's-on-the-Bouwerie, New York, imparted the news to my friend, S.T.H., that there was only room for two in his graveyard.

There are two vaults left in St. Mark's-on-the-Bouwerie,
There are two vaults left to bury the dead,
O when the two vaults are filled in St. Mark's-on-the-Bouwerie,
How will the dead bury their dead?

For Justice they are shrewdly killing the proletarian,
For Justice they are shrewdly shooting him dead,
Good Heavens, when the vaults are filled in St. Mark's-on-the-
       Bouwerie,
How will the dead bury their dead!

(*"I was born indeed in your dominions, but your service was hard, and your wages such as a man could not live on"*—Pilgrim's Progress.)

8

    And to paradise which is a port
    And over water-trestle,
    And as over a sea so over: and by the way
        of this train's movement

    Water-staves,
    Moorings, spread blue coats of water,
    Long,
    Along,
    Long.

9

A dying away as of trees
　　　where a hill-street pavement
　　　is broken into rocks:

A car sounds,

　　　Climbs.
　　　Empty, late Saturday.

At the bottom of the grade
　　　stopped short in one's rounds
　　　this tree-dying night of hurrying towards Sunday,
　　　　　uptorn by an empty trolley's rumble on usual
　　　　　　　　　　　　　　　　pursuits,
　　　　　retreats to meet
　　　　　street after empty street,
　　　　　hills paved, rising to be climbed,
　　　　　and what for houses but for windows?
　　　　　sure forecast of ongrowing moonlight.

10

　　　Passing tall
　　　Who walk upon the green
　　　So light they are not heard
　　　If never seen;—

　　　Willow above in spring haze,
　　　Green sprig and pendulous;—
　　　Wind, white lightning
　　　In branches over us;

　　　Sun;
　　　All weathering changing loves,
　　　In the high grass (kiss!)
　　　Will not uncover us.

11

Stubbing the cloud-fields—the searchlight, high
In the roseate twilight of rain-sky, green! green spring
In the heavens mild in the spring; or down suddenly
Earthwards, plunge deep suddenly earthwards,
Like escape, stampede of cattle horns, ghastly, ghastly
Their giant heads invisible for joy, grief, cavalcade,
                        plunge earthwards,
And into our hearts, O sacrifice,
But we emerge! (emerge upon a level roof that fronts
                        the sky,
The skylight of your room to rear,)
So we can breathe, the rain air and the spring
Ours, till again it moves along the sky
Down or up, machine-rayed, powerful!

12

Millennium of sun—
Beast of the field,—
Kissing the beast upon both ears—

O who will pluck geranium
With smiles before this ass's face
And tie it to his cranium
To match the ass's grace!

13

We are crossing the bridge now.
I can feel it by the sound
The wheels make over the waters.
To-night we cannot see
From the windows. But there are lights
Of two shores. And if you open the door
The water-wind blows in the brume
Which covers us.

14

Only water—

We seek of the water
The water's love!

Shall we go again
Breast to water-breast,

Gather the fish-substance,
The shining fire,
The phosphor-subtlety?

We sing who were many in the South,
At each live river mouth
Sparse-lighted, carried along!

15

And looking to where shone Orion,
Wickson—"The miracle were done
If she were to bear my son.

"As to taste there's no dispute.
But who is he may taste?
These miles of beach—
Coarse grass and ocean waste—

"Where on them can I get,
Or from their green of stars,
Something like a cucumber?"

16

Aubade, 1925

Kick the blanket away,
The man of darkness has sweated enough!
One, two, three efforts, and he stands on his feet—
Chilled a little on the cold sands.

Day. Still he is blinking man,
But eyes open: he sees
The sea, little waves, waves of the morning pearl-gray!

Agh! running the wind!

But think with the head!
This is the state of man
To raise his ashes to the dawn.
Jump, away from the coast-guard house,
Across one, two, three—! Sand mounds,

And a swamp,
Crosses of wood, newspapers in coarse island grass,
Behind a hill to be as simple as the horses.

Who has seen, who can, and who will ever see?
No one about but flat island sand and flat blue sky and
      a few mounds
Behind which—the sea, its reverberations.
Whence, if ever, then, will come sympathy?
Surely not out of the sun, nor out of the sky,
Nor out of eternity of flat island sand a little lowly to
      the aspect of eternal morning.

                Orbed sun! great air! slow time!
                The man of darkness
                Is his own monument,
                Moving his return—

Bah-h! so much blanket again—
Tousled hair—sleep!

Swims!
Spewing and spewn on to the land!
                The sun is hot!

17

      Cars once steel and green, now old,
      Find their grave at Cedar Manor.
      They rust in a wind
      The sky alone can hold.

      For the wind
      Flows heavily thru the mind like cold,
      Drums in the ears
      Till one knows its being which soon is not.

18

Tall and singularly dark you pass among the breakers—
Companionship as of another world bordering on this;
To the intelligence fastened by the senses you are lost
In a world of sunlight where nothing is amiss:

For nothing but the sun is there and peace vital with the sun,
The heaviest changes shift through no feature more than a smile,
Currents spread, and are gone, and as the high waves appear,
You dive, in the calming are as lost awhile.

How in that while intelligence escapes from sense
And fear with hurled human might darkens upon bliss!
Till as again you stand above the waters
Fear turns to sleep as one who dreamt of falling, an abyss!

19

Run on, you still dead to the sound of a name:
Climb, white froth, as on stems of flowers;

Pass near the curve of the heavens.
Sunned your whiteness is of winter frost.

For you, froth, the surge of blue-sweeping autumn,
Run to the gate of the snowed winter tomb
Where none ask why the death nor for whom;

Where the sun, too, grows small and of winter—
Drifted fruit, rotten.—

20

Close your eyes,
                    the sun low—upon them

Sky grows down, one petal
Daisy petal, broad, luminous.
A wind that makes for blindness—
                    Sun

21

O sleep, the sky goes down behind the poplars,
I scrape the gravel with my shoes and toe
The ties:
The milky moon is in the clearing,
Only the power-plant hurries in winter.

22

Cactus rose-mauve and gray, twin overturned
            natural play-paniers
in a burnt little earthen pot, green mortuary
            of plainness.
Cactus minus the red bud flower,
and the same day
            nescience of treading knee deep in snow,
always mortmain the oblivion of her
            in the desert of my traces—
Hannah, "grace." Grace under the moon,
            on blue velvet cloth I placed the prickly plant.

Think of snow.
Know duration.
All once grafted hers go to her,
            the plants, too, unseen continuance.

23

Song Theme

*To the last movement of Beethoven's Quartet
in C Sharp Minor*

All my days—
And all my ways—
Met by hands—
And ringed with feet—
Into laurel-branch the hands
Are gone, into fertile soil the feet;
  So these praised ones that are fallen off
  Are a signal in the trees,
  Are a beacon in the sun,—

Sun and death and stir, and death's
       unlit love,—
All their days
And all their ways.

24

tam cari capitis

I

Unlovely you called yourself
And at once I felt I was never lovely:
I, who had few truths to go to
Found you doubting what I loved.

Now I make you lovely my own way.
Unmentioned were we certain
Of a greater, in small assurances
Others may find trivial:

37

II

The same in all weathers.

And not till there is an end to singing
Will you go,
As you have always gone, quiet.

But like your birds that wake in the night
To sleep again:

25

Like the oceans, or the leaves of fine Southern
        palm, we must appear numbered
                to you, like the tides

Reaching up to you, also as leaves, calm, night-green,
        arching under you,
                Moon. And, O moon,
As we travail to sleep we do not know whether, with your
        genius furthering us,
We should be counted as the cuspid waves of the seas, or
        as the souls of trees
Whose leaves we are, growing for you, the crowded
        summits stark, heavenly.

26

Ask of the sun
and it may tell you—

if it will come
if it has come

that afternoon
of afternoons

when you'll have ended
shaping a plaything

circus horse of glass
a mane of beads

since art's high effort
vying with the sun's heat

shadows small—
when rather like thick peasants

out of Brueghel
after working

you stretch out—
the sun among

the hayricks of Its fields
and artless find time.

27

Blue light is the night harbor-slip.
If a number are gold they make a crown for the shore.
If three rise vertically, as one nethermost, another
                    over that, another topping,
All as if reaching, the vessel is making headway.

The scarf-pins of night-outers are sometimes that way
And, God's sky! if the body of something deploys one
                    gold light for'ard,
And, shy, a smile, may it be named? another gold light
                                        as trailer,
The general 'it is after midnight' may be a marriage,
                    or a return from the month's ball.

            Masquerade, Mozart,
            Filigree—they used to—

            (We had such a nice time)

Red! look out for this island!

Blue! and it hurts the eyes, metallic-glass this
                    beacon-light, many-faceted

It is generally safer here because,
                    in the white-washed ceiling hulk,
                    not only sparse lights for the deck
                    but life-belts

Danger! The general effect of gray light in darkness
                    is a man-of-war

Red!

Out far again
Lights—a branch laid on the world—
Their intermittence—

(We look abroad openly)

28 & 29

Two Dedications

Tibor Serly

Red varnish
Warm flitch

Of cello,
They play

Scroll before
Them—Sound

Breaks the
Sunset!—Kiss

With wide
Eyes—With

Their music
The (no?)

Pit, weather
Of tears

Which plagues
Us—Bodies

Of waves
Whose crests

Spear air,
Here rolls

The sea—
Go chase

It—a
Salt pact

Ranged over
Bars—white

Ribs pervade
In constant

Measures the
Rounds—Its

Wet frosting,
A kiss

Opens nothing,
Bend head

No! lips
Not this

An assumed
Poise among

Crowds! Blue—
Withdraws sunset—

Tones sound—
Pluck—dissonant—

Stops sing
The welter

D.R.

Comrade D.R.—
His murals speak:
Executives of industry,

Rich stone heads
Conferring at tables,
We peasants and

Workers, our faces
Becoming us more
Than frescoes of saints,

Marshal to say:
We are the
Heads over industry.

Our children, (backs
Pretty as lady bugs,
Red upon gold

Soil) now humbled
On stumps, grow
Up on soil

Turning black thru
Our efforts—water,
Our biceps, unspared.

Our mates, their mothers,
Shall know them—
Unflattered by dynamos—

Controlled among wheels
And controlling the
Glancing of belts

Against pulleys, Holidays—
There'll be many—
Will find friends

Rangers among palm
Leaf and tiger
Paw.

      Sunday; the
Miner's lantern unlit,
Coal beneath sun.

29 SONGS

1

Madison, Wis.,
remembering the bloom of Monticello (1931)

No empty bed blues—
    between these walls
I can lie—
    your thigh, me—

"Keep in it deer,
    rabbits, pigeons"—
"the figure will be better
    placed in this,"—

"Form a couch of moss"—
    queer guy
Tom Jefferson—all daughters
    no son

Sure, if you wish
    we can
turn the small Alleghenies
    to upper Japan—

But if Mr. citizen
    sells apples
in New York by
    the sea

Maybe that's
    where we
should be—
    I'll die—

The heart all
    a queen's
the brain
    Lenin's—

Empty Bed
    Blues—"keep the
thorn constantly
    wed."

2

Immature Pebbles

*An Imponderable is an article of make-believe which has become
axiomatic by force of settled habit. It can accordingly cease to be
an Imponderable by a course of unsettling habit.*
                                        —THORSTEIN VEBLEN

There are several robins here,
their legs among the triple buds—
the spring is yet too brisk
for water suds, (bathers' dirt):
instead, where the trees almost
into the water grow—below them
over the split moistened stones, ripples
make for? An observer's irrelevancy
                        of April.
Following: May.

Should then this repeated objectless
of inconsequence, following and May
bring the expected to the accustomed
in this place,
the surprise will, it can be seen, not exceed
legs of young men and women
bathing in a lake—
summer's inaction colored hot—
blue and crimson of their shivering suits
among the trees, no less ironic than what male,
encaged mandrill's blue and crimson
secret parts?

46

Observer, then, come get one going,
before one's an accessory to these ways,
obliged to accept "imponderables"—
those axioms of settling habits
no less, no more, attractive than a lake's inclusions—
pebbles, young humans . . .
In our day, impatience
handles such matters of photography
more pertinently from a train window.

3

Prop. LXI

(The Strength of The Emotions—Ethica ordine
geometrico demonstrata: IV)

Confute leaf-
Point's water with slight dropped sounds,—
Turn coat, cheat facts, say for the spring's bloom's fall
The tree's trunk has set the circling horn-branch
To cipher each drop—the eye—shot in the rain around.

So cheated well
Let the fallen bloom-wet clutter down, and into . . .
And the heart (fact . .) holds nothing, desire is
No excess, the eye points each leaf
The brain desire, the rain (cheat.) recites their brief.

4

Train-Signal

With stars past troughs to sound
—thru thick twilight
—by the stumps of the trees
blasts near the faces of leaves
by a hair's breadth separated:

with but a proof to the leaves'
closeness: leaf over leaf's face
with a hair: and the cheek kissed
with the shredded space.

5

It's a gay li - ife

There's naw—thing
        lak po—ee try
it's a delicacy
        for   a horse:

Dere's na—thing
        lak pea-   nut-brittle
it's a delicacy
        for   the molars.

6

—"her soil's birth"

(Madison)

Virtue in that—
If fall of pods' spring-seed to earth,
    Sun, ferns rise at,
Together glassed themselves in green, girth
With the windfall of her soil's birth.

    Rays sent from glass
Sphering with its beamed fall the air
    Could not surpass—
Designed to meet opposed beams there—
The unsealing of the eyes bare.

    Explosions such
As these are not for eyes to prink:
    Pods' fall too much
Inevitable, each pod will sink
Its green into a glass we drink.—

    Spring's air! which keeps
The sharpest rays of sun askew—
    Over pods sweeps:
Flecks green her hands—like ferns' virtue
In the sun keeping their green true.

7

Who endure days like this
with me   the room's inference
foghorns' tuned discs amiss
dropped our wrists would be
seconds   impatience' stem
gestures' graft   arms difference
eyes' blue iris splicing them

8

Happier, happier, now
For whom in snowsleet barberries see;
    If not that, if not that, how
Are red berries for their windsleights free?
The glaze of mind, winter of eyes,
    Snow's berries, meet!
The Void of mind, the fall of thighs,
    Cold winds heat.

Yellow flowers dead, green of leaves
Still green, look out of what eyes in love's Void?
    The close, the unseeing and unseen,
The glaze of sight snowsleet has destroyed.
Windblown, for all barberries not dead
    See with love's tear,—
The fall of thighs; love's discrete forehead
    Happier.

9

In Arizona
      (how many years in the mountains)
The small stumped bark of a tree
Looks up
      in the shape of an adored pup

The indians do not approach it
The round indian tents
      remain where they are
The tanned whites
      are never seen by it
And one can imagine its imploring eyes

The skies
      it seems to look up to
          blue
The same sun that warms the desert
Warms what one
      can imagine to be its ears.

10

Arizona

arch animals'
upearthed faces—
dust of
their red, wrinkled—

higher than the oil wells
are the rocks—
the fluted cactus, its
spiked needle locks,

rasp shard in
the blue air, blood boil
into the unprofitable
eiffel towers of oil

11

Home For Aged Bomb Throwers—U.S.S.R.

When is winter, spring?
When, tho ice is not breaking,
One has what one does not expect
    to be taking

It is against the winds
It is against firm ice
But with the sun, that
                falling asleep
Winter is spring

1/6 of the earth

12

Whatever makes this happening
    Is unheard
    To a third.

Two. Where two should
    Stand. One. One.
    With the sun. In a wood.

Tomorrow is unsought.
    No oasis of ivy to inurn
    Either foot or fern.

13

in that this happening
        is not unkind
it put to
        shame every kindness

mind, mouths, their words
        people, put sorrow
           on
        its body

before sorrow it came
        and before every kindness,
happening for every sorrow
        before every kindness;

14

The sand: For the cigarette finished
on the beach the universal ash-tray:

or where the bacon grease is spilt:
Knowledge: smell is taken up

and off by the seas'
winds:

        a ship's
funnel is seen from this house
and rain drenches a witness of departure:

love as the relaxation among breakers
a dog-carcass—its wet—a reminder:

15

Do not leave me
    before that convert surfeit
which if it ever leaves toward you—
    never to your misgiving—
        inexistent
comes first to me in another

That surfeit—other—which
    much less you do not look for, distraction
from this our being together
    never surfeit—the owned
devolving upon—owned—and neither owned—

That distraction which neither of us
    much less you, close, seeks—love
never prior to your patience
    asks that surfeit come upon me first—
unowned misgiving;

it is but a mouth's mumblings:
    no distraction coming
after love, convert
    of your patience—a mouth knowing;
close, its unowned owner.

16

Crickets'
thickets

light,
delight:

sleeper's eyes,
keeper's;

      Plies!
lightning

frightening
whom . . . ?

doom
nowhere . . .

where eyes . . .
air,

are crickets'
air

17

Imitation*

N.Y. 1932

In the imitation of Gothic
building   and a virgin
as Virgin   her recessed space
Her alcove   its "statue"   a quadrangle
stones considered built   imitation

within a court   a garden   bluebells
in New York City   imitation of
a chalet   set apart for meals
familiar to Americans if not the Swiss

this institution   by deliberateness   of engraving
THE ACADEMY OF THE HOLY CHILD
to which dedicated from up
the rich street hurries   promised   young
the academician and wholly child
all his attention religiously kept by vast
cubic contents of gas tank built on principles of
a steel erector set given him by his aunt
just off the boat from Pekin   coloration of sea
plate steel rectangles mirrored blue at the water-line
the gas tank walls   the same composition   same color

—Xavier   you know, or have not you heard
in China even comparatively recently
the physicians attending women of the upper
class never saw their patients but for
a hand extended from behind a screen
for the taking of their pulse   and so   depended
for the rest of the diagnoses upon a proxy
a small carved figure of a woman
sometimes of ivory upon which the patient indicated
the approximate location of her complaint

other Chinese ivories   tablets which were held
in front of their mouths by officials
when they had audience   certain leaves
fall long crisp like red halved sausages
roasted to a turn this autumn for the sidewalks
of New York of the occupants of the taxis
of the imitation of wealth thru the exhaust
girdle pendants   back scratchers with ivory handles
cages for singing and fighting crickets

* Imitation: *Mus.* The repetition of a phrase or subject in another
voice-part or in a different key.

56

18

The mirror oval sabres   playing

at chips in the room

next door   the voices behind the wall

will be lit by high lights in the morning

in bed a wall between continuing voices

chips stacking   instead of bales

the water sounds extending a harbor

one sleepless one sleeper on the fourth floor

19

Checkers, checkmate and checkerboard,
Confused are *checkerboard* and *chess*;
Shall whose writing be on paper
Whose move is on the checkerboard?

If red of a set have each a wreath
Each black checker should be wreathed:
Noble typing will make the writing
Her breath is his, to type "checkmate bequeathed."

20

Ears beringed with fuzz

owned a man's sculpturing head

autumn's regard

for weather like spring

holed shoes meeting pavement

If, when,

introduce these to

a fuzzed flower   Petal will

declare as of carving   "bluish soles'

walk, head, ears' hair: greeting"

21

Snows' night's winds on the window rattling
Would seem to leap out of the bed-spring

What prevents a feat like that occurring
Reason—but the more actual bedding

Springs of steel mercurial spirallings
Making a body's night a changeable singing

The winged boots of the frozen seek of it! sheltering
Safety from the window's pommelling

To my wash-stand
in which I wash
my left hand
and my right hand

To my wash-stand
whose base is Greek
whose shaft
is marble and is fluted

To my wash-stand
whose wash-bowl
is an oval
in a square

To my wash-stand
whose square is marble
and inscribes two
smaller ovals to left and right for soap

Comes a song of
water from the right faucet and the left
my left and my
right hand mixing hot and cold

Comes a flow which
if I have called a song
is a song
entirely in my head

a song out of imagining
modillions descried above
my head   a frieze
of stone completing what no longer

is my wash-stand
since its marble has completed

my getting up each morning
my washing before going to bed

my look into a mirror
to glimpse half an oval
        as if its half
were half-oval in my head   and the

climates of many
inscriptions human heads shapes'
        horses' elephants' (tusks) others'
scratched in marble tile

so my wash-stand
in one particular breaking of the
        tile at which I have
looked and looked

has opposed to my head
the inscription of a head
        whose coinage is the
coinage of the poor

observant in waiting
in their getting up mornings
        and in their waiting
going to bed

carefully attentive
to what they have
        and to what they do not
                have

when a flow of water
        doubled in narrow folds
occasions invertible counterpoints
        over a head   and

an age in a wash-stand
and in their own heads

23

"The Immediate Aim"

I

Other than propaganda—

a police dog sniffs one;
a *German* police dog
not responsible for Naziism?
One is not sweet on him.

When one does not love animals,
one's concern is not respect.

Workers,
you could
take time off
this March morning

trot out
like this police dog

ambling critic
of spring

(the curse of verse on him!)

might make bare your eyes
to the white gull
astigmatically a launch

since it sits, distant
in the middle of the river:

your value which enslaves you
in advance

has made your eye-pupils limited—

inanity
to prate
the injustice of it.

2

Can dogs
argue
injustices

Dogs in a vise,
and a wood saw
can saw an anatomy
of dog

Such as you never saw.

If it yowls
shut the eyelid on a bad dream,
Let not the snarls take,
With its virus in you
You are immune.

What hounds
you means to.
Not all woodsawyers
grow animal.

3

Shanty
on the river
with
one window

The unemployed
having
a home
has no home

and no nag
protected
by
the United States' flag—

each animal
his own gravedigger
almost
sings

who will
walk out
against
the

social
and political
order of
things

24

This Fall, 1933

THE AMERICAN BANKNOTE FACTORY
        makes bills
The lights are on thru its basement,
        10 times 10 squared down the windows of its façade.

A boy with a rabbit in hand could no more
Caress it for his benumbed fingers, than if
        The drafts from the outside blew in noon and midnight,

Stormed green bills on the fall's leaves, the bills
Could caress them, make New York pavement less
        Bereavement, heyday out of moneyed inflation.

25
No One Inn

P.S.   i.e.   almost dreamt
the face against the door
a pastel's   a boy's

who owns it   being in a war
plays the market early
hires a chef   would look at his chef's hat

flour not at the exchange of
the exchanges   the margin drops
gets the chef walking   and preparing

it a cork   please,
be it, whose thought is it
floated   and by a house-boat

if there   wound 's sleep, to be sure
"then bacteria in mercurochrome?"—yes
if you want peroxide I will give you—thrive

the windings   an inn
the windings   a face in an inn
the windings   no one is in in No One Inn

26

A Junction

To such of one body as one mind

Whose ear shouts to ear separation,

Across the mean levels of oceans,

Cities,—

To them a sight thru windows

Which will not last,

The heart, and an arm—if it should conduct

Remembering.

27

Song—¾ time
(pleasantly drunk)

Right out
of
Das Kapital

vol. I
chap. 3
2.
A

"who has
a
taste

"for something
that will
warm
up"

snow
    for
        my friend's birthday

I've
    been climbing
           every
              little

highway
        snow without—
              He

dances
    it
     —without—
           any money

(his
    friend's
        nose

is
 at
  the
    window

for the
    snow
        sparrows

in the
    junk
      heap
        of snow)

with
   a
   girl

over
   every
      little
         highway

of
  Spain
      for—

"there
      develops
            a
               multiplicity

"of
   social
         relations

"that are
         spontaneous in
                     their
                         growth

"and are
         quite
               outside

"the
      control of
               the
                  actors"

"When
      one commodity
                  replaces another

"the
   money
         commodity
                  always

"remains
		in
			the hands

"of
	some
		third
			person"

"Circulation
			sweats money
					unceasingly

"at every pore."
				"because the
						weaver has sold
								linen;

"the distiller
			is only able to
					sell the strong

"waters
		because the
				bible agent has already

"sold the waters
			of

			—

				life;

"and
	so
		on."

28

"Specifically, a writer of music." The composite of notes proceeded with assumed qualities in a definite proportion. But, as dreamed, they controlled the nature of plants, bodies, etc., and the elements of the notes became not easy to separate. And, on the large muscle of the back, which passes from the spine to the head, they were settling longitudinally, like the wings of certain insects, where in the large opening of the roof in the ancient house stood the air.

He stood and turned the palm of the hand downward and backward, and like the notes the movement was extended in time. This act became a test of his powers. His body was published abroad, and like the Titan, long after him, whose liver renewed itself at night, it renewed itself on a long promenade in the mornings of days, the notes always the principal effort of his performance. He saw no one—only flowers, branches and buds developing from unusual places.

Till where the stamens combined by their filaments to form two bundles, he saw her, the power of authority upon her head. But her crown was a crown of his notes, so that she was immediately separate from him, as the notes were separate from her in what seemed to him their conversation in which she did yet did not take part. She disappeared into the brush.

And he heard himself saying, "For, I am at least half blind, my windows are all as full of glasses of waters as any mountebanks stall" on a field crowded with dancing donkeys. Half-crazed, he was running into them, seeking always the daughter of the governor of Seville. Stamping over him, the hoofs of the donkeys delivered, themselves delivered, the body of Don Giovanni to the devil. And as the field was impaired upon the point of their receding vision, the ever falling stomping of their hoofs, now following the range of his notes, were imparting to him clearly: "Sir, not only a mathematique point flowers into every line which is derived from a Center, but our soul which is but one, hath swallowed up a negative."

And now a dancing-master named Fox, but very gentle,—the music becoming a shallow, rounded depression. Gentle, and an irritant almost hard to be conscious of. So that the simplest fact of his life, "specifically, a writer of music," was beginning to mean very little. And for years it was four o'clock,—not time which would have broken the hour and placed a statue of David

in history, but an ornamental herb of that name,—with flowers
that grow in Peru of a great variety of color. So that for years it
was four o'clock and the same as bloom from 4 P.M. till the next
morning. And since there was a memory of the hoofs of donkeys
who had left him, there could now be the sum of three and one,
and of twice two. The groups came in four units: a team of four
horses, a playing card with four spots, quadrupled measures, a
bedstead with four posts, a four-wheeler allowing passage in anyone of four directions. Golf for a foursome. In rows of townships,
six miles in width, between two meridian lines, isolated groups
composed of sympathetic individuals who had given free play to
all the feelings and passions had reached the doldrums of Fourier-
ism, but without success. In their hearths the phosphorescence of
foxwood, and he was a bystander. They were foxtrotting, two
couples and four friends, two friends and four couples, between
a pace and a walk, between a pace and a walk. He could see the
upper-leather of their shoes along the edges next the soles. They
moved very gently and sadly.

He was in his own time, his fears too much aroused and prolonged, teased by repeated disappointments in the attainment of
his object. If his notes could not extricate themselves from this
complicated mass, they would be to his tactility like meeting at
a point without further coincidence or intersection. If they did
extricate themselves, they would, moving towards a definite shape,
become capable of being apprehended, themselves their own existence in the plain of surrounding existence, tactility of materials
become tangible. Lao-tse was working a Chinese puzzle consisting
of a square cardboard cut by straight incisions into five triangles,
a square and a lozenge—combining them into a variety of figures.
It was a relief from ethics, an approach to the blue huckleberry.
The tap-dancer was not a Chinaman. He was in a trench plunged
to his neck in water, the fruit hanging above him. On a level with
it a caterpillar tractor was pecking away at an acre of earth.
Foolish, but there was the tap-dancer singing:

Taps nailed upon the heel of shoe
Make the water tantivy, tantivy, tantivy

Then he danced out very clearly and swiftly:

My instep in the stirrup's
tapadera

The tap-dancer was tapering towards the head, in a column of
water growing conical, around, and containing, him. He heard a
woman using a medicine composed of an ingredient of tansy say:
One of the principal applications of tannic acid is in the prepara-
tion of writing-ink. He turned the tap-dance into a tango passing
out in a diagonal shuffle.

Whirl, dip, and a swing! The duenna is a dragon! What is it, inflexible Draco, that is fabulous, has wings unlike a serpent, and is a monster! Come on! Come on! drag your brains! The Northern constellation? Guess again! A short, large-bored firearm of the 17th century or the soldier who carried it? That was before your time, what do you know about it? The small arboreal Asiatic lizard (genus *Draco*!) leaps aided by a parachute formed by lateral expansions of the skin supported by elongated and extensible hind ribs. What shall we say of the little flying lizards, what of the metamorphosis of the dragonfly, its four large wings and enormous eyes? Shall we call them with fourfold-thought of gentleness the devil's darning needle. The dragon is a duenna! The dragon has an inner paddle-shaft like a marine engine! The dragon is an excavator that draws the soil upward and away from the working-base thus clearing it. Scripturally, *tannim*, the meaning of which is uncertain. There went up a smoke out of his nostrils, and fire out of his mouth devoured: coals were kindled by it.—Wounds stink.—Caused men to ride over our heads. As smoke is driven away, so drive them away. (To the chief Musician, Psalms 18, 38, 66, 68!)

29
N.Y.

"At heaven's gate" the larks: have
Read to date the nth reversion, "re" Marx

Of the mind's image   a hangar
A red crane—on the nearby wharves

In the spring-blue day—not working
But not out of languor

January the 29 , the 29th birthday
Falling on a Sunday

As planned there should be to-day
29 songs written over two years

And with, but without expected, pay

I have written down twenty-three
Leaving 5 and another page blank

To record a January without snow
For the delectation of the file and rank.

"Further than"—

Further than the wash-stand
three mountains in one bathroom
The mountains on the floor, sea-bed
rock, colored design; Five figures, chance
smudges, perhaps tar, in the mountains; Six
and Five figures in the waters under
and above them. Each figure
is an ordinate of which the axis

is a peak, The Whole Peak, from summit
thru base to inverted altitude, depth beneath
sea level. Only drying from the shower is
exploration possible, the chances
of world monopoly have been so carefully
seized that only on the other side of
one's bathroom nothing is foreign. Unless
charting the antarctic has something to do
with figures the heads of which are
just smudges away from the axis of abscissas
or one is merely exploring from a shower
expectant that today or tomorrow must
bring the new economic anatomization.

"Mantis"

Mantis! praying mantis! since your wings' leaves
And your terrified eyes, pins, bright, black and poor
Beg—"Look, take it up" (thoughts' torsion)! "save it!"
I who can't bear to look, cannot touch,—You—
You can—but no one sees you steadying lost
In the cars' drafts on the lit subway stone.

Praying mantis, what wind-up brought you, stone
On which you sometimes prop, prey among leaves
(Is it love's food your raised stomach prays?), lost
Here, stone holds only seats on which the poor
Ride, who rising from the news may trample you—
The shops' crowds a jam with no flies in it.

Even the newsboy who now sees knows it
No use, papers make money, makes stone, stone,
Banks, "it is harmless," he says moving on—You?
Where will he put *you*? There are no safe leaves
To put you back in here, here's news! too poor
Like all the separate poor to save the lost.

Don't light on my chest, mantis! do—you're lost,
Let the poor laugh at my fright, then see it:
My shame and theirs, you whom old Europe's poor

73

Call spectre, strawberry, by turns; a stone—
You point—they say—you lead lost children—leaves
Close in the paths men leave, saved, safe with you.

Killed by thorns (once men), who now will save you
Mantis? what male love bring a fly, be lost
Within your mouth, prophetess, harmless to leaves
And hands, faked flower,—the myth is: dead, bones, it
Was assembled, apes wing in wind: On stone,
Mantis, you will die, touch, beg, of the poor.

Android, loving beggar, dive to the poor
As your love would even without head to you,
Graze like machined wheels, green, from off this stone
And preying on each terrified chest, lost
Say, I am old as the globe, the moon, it
Is my old shoe, yours, be free as the leaves.

Fly, mantis, on the poor, arise like leaves
The armies of the poor, strength: stone on stone
And build the new world in your eyes, Save it!

"*Mantis*," *An Interpretation*

or Nomina sunt consequentia rerum,
names are sequent to the things named

Mantis! praying mantis! since your wings' leaves
        Incipit Vita Nova
        le parole . . .
        almeno la loro sentenzia
the words . . .
at least their substance

at first were
"The mantis opened its body
It had been lost in the subway
It steadied against the drafts
It looked up—
Begging eyes—

74

It flew at my chest"

      —The ungainliness
      of the creature needs stating.

No one would be struck merely
By its ungainliness,
Having seen the thing happen.

Having seen the thing happen,
There would be no intention 'to write it up,'

But *all* that was happening,
The mantis itself only an incident, *compelling any writing*
The transitions were perforce omitted.

Thoughts'—two or three or five or
Six thoughts' reflection (pulse's witness) of what was happening
All immediate, not moved by any transition.

Feeling this, what should be the form
Which the ungainliness already suggested
Should take?

      —Description—lightly—ungainliness
      With a grace unrelated to its surroundings.

Grace there is perhaps
In the visual sense, not in the movement of
"eyes, pins, bright, black and poor."

Or considering more than the isolation
Of one wrenched line,

Consider:
"(thoughts' torsion)"
la battaglia delli diversi pensieri . . .
the battle of diverse thoughts—
The actual twisting
Of many and diverse thoughts

What form should *that* take?
　　　—The first words that came into mind
　　　"The mantis opened its body—"
　　　Which might deserve the trope:
　　　the feeling of the original which is a permanence

　　　?

Or the feeling accompanying the first poor 27 words' inception
(the original which is a permanence
?),
That this thoughts' torsion
Is really a sestina
Carrying subconsciously
Many intellectual and sensual properties of the
　　　　　forgetting and remembering Head
One human's intuitive Head

　　　　　Dante's rubric
　　　　　Incipit
　　　　　Surrealiste
　　　　　Re-collection

A twisted shoe by a pen, an insect, lost,
"To the short day and the great sweep of shadow."

The sestina, then, the repeated end words
Of the lines' winding around themselves,
Since continuous in the Head, whatever has been read,
　　　　　whatever is heard,
　　　　　　whatever is seen
Perhaps goes back cropping up again with
Inevitable recurrence again in the blood
Where the spaces of verse are not visual
But a movement,
With vision in the lines merely a movement.

What is most significant
Perhaps is that C—and S—and X—of the 19th century
Used the "form"—not the form but a Victorian
Stuffing like upholstery

For parlor polish,
And our time takes count against them
For their blindness and their (unintended?) cruel smugness.

Again: as an experiment, the sestina would be wicker-work—
As a force, one would lie to one's feelings not to use it

One feels in fact inevitably
About the coincidence of the mantis lost in the subway,
About the growing oppression of the poor—
Which is the situation most pertinent to us—,
With the fact of the sestina:
Which together fatally now crop up again
To twist themselves anew
To record not a sestina, post Dante,
Nor even a mantis.

Is the poem then, a sestina
Or not a sestina?

The word sestina has been
Taken out of the original title. It is no use (killing oneself?)

        —Our world will not stand it,
        the implications of a too regular form.

Hard to convince even one likely to show interest in the matter
That this regularity to which 'write it up' means not a damn

(Millet in a Dali canvas, Circe in E's Cantos)
Whatever seeming modelling after the event,
649 years, say, after Dante's first canzone,
If it came back immediately as the only
Form that will include the most pertinent subject of our day—
The poor—
Cannot mean merely implied comparison, unreality
Usually interpreted as falsity.

Too much time cannot be saved
Saying:
The mantis might have heaped up upon itself a
Grave of verse,

But the facts are not a symbol.

There is the difference between that
And a fact (the mantis in the subway)
And all the other facts the mantis sets going about it.

No human being wishes to become
An insect for the sake of a symbol.

But the mantis *can start*
History etc.
The mantis situation remains its situation,
Enough worth if the emotions can equate it,

"I think" of the mantis
"I think" of other things—
The quotes set repulsion
Into movement.

Repulsion—
Since one, present, won't touch the mantis,
Will even touch the poor—

but carefully.

The mantis, then,
Is a small incident of one's physical vision
Which is the poor's helplessness
The poor's separateness
Bringing self-disgust.

The mantis is less ungainly than that.

There should be to-day no use for a description of it
Only for a "movement" emphasizing its use, since it's been around,

An accident in the twisting
Of many and diverse "thoughts"
i.e. nerves, glandular facilities, electrical cranial charges
For example—
line 1—entomology
line 9—biology

78

lines 10 and 11—the even rhythm of riding under-
          ground, and the sudden jolt are also
          of these nerves, glandular facilities,
          brain's charges
line 12—pun, fact, banality
lines 13 to 18—the economics of the very poor—the
          newsboy—unable to think beyond
          "subsistence still permits competi-
          tion," banking, *The Wisconsin Elkhorn
          Independent*—"Rags make paper,
          paper makes money, money makes
          banks, banks make loans, loans make
          poverty, poverty makes rags."
lines 22 to 24—Provence myth
lines 25 to 29—Melanesian self-extinction myth
line 33—airships
lines 35 and 36—creation myth (Melanesia), residue of
          it in our emotions no matter if fetched
          from the moon, as against l. 25 to 29.
and naturally the coda which is the
only thing that can sum up the
jumble of order in the lines weaving
"thoughts," pulsations, running commentary, one upon the other,
itself a jumble of order
as far as poetic
sequence is concerned:

      the mantis
      the poor's strength
      the new world.

29—"in your eyes"
      the original shock still persisting—

So that the invoked collective
Does not subdue the senses' awareness,
The longing for touch to an idea, or
To a use function of the material:
The original emotion remaining,
    like the collective,
Unprompted, real, as propaganda.

The voice exhorting, trusting what one hears
Will exhort others, is the imposed sensuality of an age

When both propaganda and sensuality are necessary against—
"—we have been left with nothing
just a few little unimportant ships
and barges" (British Admiralty even in 1920)

or jelly for the Pope

la mia nemica, madonna la pieta
my enemy, my lady pity,

36—"like leaves"
The Head remembering these words exactly in the way it
                                                    remembers
la calcina pietra
the calcined stone.

But it remembers even more constantly
the poor
than
com' huom pietra sott' erba
as one should hide a stone in grass.

Nor is the coincidence
Of the last four lines
Symbolism,
But the simultaneous,
The diaphanous, historical
In one head.

November 4, 1934
New York

The six blank pages intended by Song 29, written January 29th, 1933, were filled during 1933 and the early months of 1934 with songs 11, 23, 24, 26, 27, 28. Added to the original collection their number is not included in, or for, the title of the book, namely *55 Poems*. They are dedicated rather by their subjects.

Anew

1

che di lor suona su nella tua vita

I walked out, before
"Break of day"
And saw
Four cabins in the hay.

Blue sealed glasses
Of preserves—four—
In the window-sash
In the yard on the bay.

Further:
The waters
At the ramp
Running away.

2

One lutenist played *look;* your thought was *drink:*
Then why like him pledge her to see?
Ben, all clocks stop in a house-party's eyes.
Music avoids impossibility.

If lonely she go with me from this room
We will look where lute notes dispose,
Whether from some rebellious dead, or still
One more earth where the marsh-marigold grows.

3

The green plant grows
Says your old man
But the white pot it is in
    Does not grow
The thorns are the roses'.

My old man's beard
Is older than your old man's,
And whatever song, the winds,
    And the snow,
Older than their prose is.

Went a lande a
Ship of Lusseboene but that lande
*. . . All thinges is comune**
    As we know
As their suns' our sons' closes.

* Amerigo Vespucci

4

So sounds grass, and if it is sun or no sun
Sun on bur, or a noise in the ear's burr
A long sleep, and a full stillness.
It is Light. Circles
           star.

        Bur,
        Sum,
If they ask, it is you
Never with wilfulness,

A high fire fills a trench.
Sum, Egypt was a Sum, knows you as
Trench mortar and pyramids.

Sum, you are constructed, as of the tides, of your voice,
Water has this constancy, illness nothing,
By cheek bones
As of two as of many in the hills of Teruel

The guns of the loyal arms
Leaving the hands hanging from branches in snow,
River bottoms
And their shores where river bottoms were.

5

Ah spring, when with a thaw of blue
Sun in the street will she be as to-day?
Seaplane up to sky over sky
Avenues without empire an earth of May.

6

Anew, sun, to fire summer
leaves move toward the air
from the stems of the branches

       fire summer   fire summer

but for the people cheated
from the birds heard singing
thru four months on shore
toward the people in the waves

the green leaves that fill up the day
and those eaten away
—point-lace worked over a stem—
blow up on the trees of the cliff

on the top
the mill with the clock-tower
fires summer
       over a midsummer shore.

7

When the crickets
sound like fifty water-taps
forsaken at once

the inclemency
of the inhuman noises
is the earth's

with its roadways
over cabins in the forests

the sheets smell
of sweet milk

all the waters
of the world

we are going
to sleep to sleep

8

Has the sum
Twenty-five
Reduced the years
Of the live songs
To one-quarter
Of a century
Become cold mortar
Of a pyramid?
        Forget the number
Think of an entablature of snow
Engraved there 2 a bird-prow
Taking 5 in tow,
Then Ra look down

The figure shining thru the measure
Each song the midday
A sum of each year's leisure.

9

For you I have emptied the meaning
Leaving the song
Or would a god—a god of midday
Have been brought in by the neck
For foes to peck at

God the man is so overweening
He would prolong
A folly of thought see 2 as a bird
And what not that we rid day of
So that we may think in our time

Two birds tip on the guy wire
The green rained on
Is coppered by sunset, a treeling's
So black (together we hush a response) between
Its trunk and silk mesh of kirtle showed evening.

10

What are these songs
straining at sense—
you the consequence?

11

In the midst of things
One scotch and soda, and
Happy birthday! have you
Been walking in DICKEYVILLE
EIGHTEENTH CENTURY
DEVELOPMENT?
They turned
The walls of an old mill
There into a house.

VOICE OF THE HOUSE-DOOR
(Speaking after Catullus):
Sees all—
Time brings the guy with red eyebrows
In love with the Mrs. of this house
Who had her husband
After she had had his father.

(Pitying itself considerably)
Dazh the nizhest poem
I ever wrote exshepting
All the other nizher poems.

12

It's hard to see but think of a sea
Condensed into a speck.
And there are waves—
Frequencies of light,
Others that may be heard.
The one is one sea, the other a second.
There are electric stresses across condensers
That wear them down till they can stand no strain,
Are of no force and as unreclaimed
            as the bottom of the sea

Unless the space the stresses cross be air,
        that can be patched.
Large and small condensers,
Passing in the one instance frequencies
        that can be turned to sound,
In the other, alternations that escape,
So many waves of a speck of sea or what,
Or a graph the curve of a wave beyond all sound,
An open circuit where no action—
Like that of the retina made human by light—
Is recorded otherwise
Than having taken a desired path a little way
And tho infinitely a mote to be uncontained for
        ever.
This science is then like gathering flowers of the
        weed
One who works with me calls birdseed
That are tiny and many on one stem
They shed to the touch tho on a par
        with the large flower
That picked will find a vase.
I see many things at one time
        the harder the concepts get,
Or nothing
Which is a forever become me over forty years.
I am like another, and another, who has
        finished learning
And has just begun to learn.
If I turn pages back
A child may as well be staring with me
Wondering at the meaning
I turn to last
Perhaps.

13

A last cigarette
a companion

dark, spring's
green smells

and the work
is in mind

a love's
unclouding it

the spontaneous
idea

is not yet
called up

a green light
of the subway
entrance

to let spring ask
is the world

at the World's Fair
any more
than an action sings.

Science, too, posted
after all smells

carefully fostering
cadres

not grudging
time

patiently
"bothering."

14

"One oak fool box";—the pun
Retrieved from past days
Will soon be quicker than the thronged
Waiting room of the terminal in the dimout
In time of war,
When three trains leave within
        a minute of each other
For the same place:—
Here simmer the stray words of friends,
Guise of an agitation of electrical storms,
The accelerated impulse and emotion
             of events
Under the immense vault with
        extinguished bulbs,
In the granite columns
That derive unwieldy acanthus:—
The pun born of an oak file,
Of an aimless card index where there
            was peace:—
Dooley said:—and not so damned mute—
When the story of a great battle is written,
They'll print the killed,
The wounded, the missing,
And the seriously disturbed:—
As if some ancient head
Or its plaster cast,
Colorless water,
Said:—
If number, measure and weighing
Be taken away from any art,
That which remains will not be much:—
At least nothing like an
Appreciation of dawn
After the sixth day of work in one week:—
Or of snow melting from trees
If it falls with a sound of leaves.

15

No it was no dream of coming death,
Those you love will live long.
If light hurried my dream, I saw none:
Stepped from my bed and to the sill,
From a window looked down
On the river I knew set forth
To rise toward me—full after rain.
People watched, crowded the banks, thought
As with old words to a river:
(*Whose waters seemed unwillingly*
to glide like friends who linger while
they sever.) Soon, as expected!
A coffin launched like a ship's hull
Sped as from a curtain afire
Draped to the keystone of an arch
And—as at a burial at sea—
Sank. The displaced water rose,
Made the heart sound the coffin's grave,
Woke under the stream and in me
A set of furtive bells, muted
And jangling by rote "What does this say?
What loss will make the world different?
Are they gathered to further war?
What sorrow do you fear?
Ask, will you, is it here
Distrust is cast off, all
Cowardice dies. Eyes, looking out,
Without the good of intellect,
Rouse as you are used to:
It is the bad fallen away,
And the sorrow in the good.
  You saw now for your book, *Anew.*"

16

I walk in the old street
to hear the beloved songs
afresh
this spring night.

Like the leaves—my loves wake—
not to be the same
or look tireless to the stars
and a ripped doorbell.

17

Guillaume de Machault (1300–1377)
Ballade: Plourès, dames

Cry for me, ladies, your servant
    Who said all he
May, I leave heart and intent,

Heart, my desire and thought, as your servant,
    To honor you
Whom God keep and augment.

        Dress yourselves in black for me,
            My heart fails my pale look (you see)
    Death is all I see of this adventure
            If God and you
    Do not take me for sure.

18

The bird that cries like a baby
Is the crow
Or a softer voice.
The turning spray of cypress
The seeming evergreen
With red falls of Virginia creeper
Nears the red of forsythia
That with the season lost its yellow.
Crickets keep filing away.
Forsythia named *Golden-rain* of parks
Appears wild in the country.
How like the west is the east
The sun setting sooner:
A tulip-tree by itself makes the autumnal east golden.
Before the clock was turned back an hour
This morning and it stopped saving daylight
A rescript was heard—
Caw—
Of the oldest Throne's baby,
"To enhance justice on earth
        and to make the world one household . . . "

Swimming in the creek
Water is colder and older.

19

And so till we have died
And grass with grass
Lie faceless as the grass

Grow sheathed with the grass
Between our spines a hollow
The stillest sense will pass
Or weighted cloud will follow.

20

The lines of this new song are nothing
But a tune making the nothing full
Stonelike become more hard than silent
The tune's image holding in the line.

21

Can a mote of sunlight defeat its purpose
When thought shows it to be deep or dark?

See sun, and think shadow.

22

Catullus viii

Miserable Catullus, stop being foolish
And admit it's over,
The sun shone on you those days
When your girl had you
When you gave it to her
        like nobody else ever will.
Everywhere together then, always at it
And you liked it and she can't say
                she didn't
Yes, those days glowed.
Now she doesn't want it: why
        should you, washed out
Want to. Don't trail her,
Don't eat yourself up alive,
Show some spunk, stand up
                and take it.

So long, girl. Catullus

                    can take it.

He won't bother you, he won't

                    be bothered:

But you'll be, nights.

What do you want to live for?

Whom will you see?

Who'll say you're pretty?

Who'll give it to you now?

Whose name will you have?

Kiss what guy? bite whose

                    lips?

Come on Catullus, you can

                    take it.

23

Gulls over a rotting hull,
Past a bridge their wings annul,
Are such fact the time must see:
Where no bridge spans war's decree,
Birds do, sea, ruin, burial.

24

The men in the kitchens
Their women in the foundries
The children in the wars
The old men at the boundaries.

25

for
Zadkine

It is a hard thing to say that when I first saw
La Prisonnière I wanted to run
And that I did, only that some birds then sang
In your courtyard, pursuing me
Over stone where you work in stone,
To come upon the prisoner in a field again.
Grass overgrowing ruins of the war
Over which she sprang, her head for other hours,
   above a wrecked column—
Like none that had ever been—
Nailed together maybe from broken curbs of wells,
   wood once now stone:
There, she was the Furies sometime called kind
Where the haunted stop on a ray of sun
Tho the bird still dreamed of pursues—
Any bird, that is, over a gravestone
Or a grave lacking one.
In the art of stone it is hard to set one's own
   seal upon the idea of stone,
And in a world from which most
   ideas have gone
To take the wreck of its idea
And make it stone
Raised up as a column
In which the prisoner is meant to be,
Over seas and fields and years,
Beside Daphne in the tree
And like a tree
But of stone to be seen in the sun,
Is harder.
There are almost no friends
But a few birds to tell what you have done.

26

1892–1941

To be moved comes of want, tho want be complete
as understanding. Cast, the statue rests, stopped:
a bronze—not "Grief"—the drapery should take in
body and head. The working eyes discarded.

Characterless lips, straight nose, sight, form no clue
(are none too great sculpture) to portrait or you.
At the seat of government, but a cab's jaunt
from the evergreens raised about the statue,

people count, climb the steps of the Capitol.
Shrubs, close to hands, that age at the visitor's
curved bench derive no clue from its smooth stone or
its simplicity or animal foot ends.

Nor shows the headstone back of the figure's seat
more than a blank emblem of two wreaths entwined,
bare in Eighteen Ninety Two, of our country.
Dark forearm not draped, hand modeled to the chin:

a lady of Nineteen Forty One met by
chance, asked where you could be found, took us three here,
left quickly, said, "The two of them lie there"

(I am one alive while two see here with me)

under the circle of purposeful gravel
feet must skirt or cross to come near the figure
over the gravel as on no other plot, in
"the cemetery known as Rock Creek": the name

gravel, those under. "One's instinct abhors time."

27

A madrigal for 3 voices

Hail the tree's meadow
Where the watch
Fees no property

    Where bread crumbs strike
      Red raked leaves
    Pigeons redden shadow
      Under red feet

        When pigeons greet
Workers meeting—
In the valley
    of the city—
Not a chimney's
    made of putty
And the lampposts
      are high
        high
          and white—or
        red, like
no property of
      night.

28

The rains, the rains
Toward spring pour thru
The winter night
And freeze to hail.

Seasoned armies
Tested in defeat
Retreating now
In that order

They cannot yield,
No more than weather
Of their hemisphere:
The rain that turns

To hail before
The thunderstorms,
The rains, the rains
Of spring call out.

29

Glad they were there
Falling away
Flying not to
Lose sight of it
Not going far
In angles out
Of ovals of
Dances filled up
The field the green
With light above
With the one hand
In the other.

30

A marriage song
for
Florence and Harry

Be happy you two
    Whose one aim
Makes the bride take
    The bridegroom's name.

As the birds on the hedge.
    Nor edge
Away in time
To ask how two
    May be
    Happy.

31

My nephew
And my new
Niece

Joy
On their wedding

From his mother
My sister
He never saw
And my mother
Her mother
Hers

    not to see

From my father
And his father

To the bride
Whatever she be

From the unconcerned
Dancers
Today

From the streets
From the walls
Of their house
Tomorrow

From where
He works

From the hills
From the sea

What if a thousand
Has been thrown
Away

Leaves of the fall
Gold

Blow away

Joy
On their wedding

Love tomorrow
Loved today

32

Even if love convey
His line, his tone,
We see him, alone,
Dissatisfied,
Tonight near yesterday.

See in his art
This tone the sun
And in this line his living eyes.
All was in place with him,
My valentine.

Even while on our green wall
His painting hangs
And makes new our will, oh
All artlessness cries:
"Sleep fast, I need the pillow!"

33

Drive, fast kisses,
no need to see
hands or eyelashes
a mouth at her ear
trees or leaves
night or the days.

34
The Letter of Poor Birds

The letter of poor birds
Is a wish or a song:
If we can be more, should we
On uninteresting land?
Today we saw hollows and low crests
The fallow, the arid, and the growing patch,
The yellow root of a red shrub
    make winter rosy
And cast such shadow on a white cottage.
The sparrows cram bread and drink. Do we
Drink more than water that flaws a drain?
You will believe they sang:
Jerry, Paul, Celia, Louis.

35
Or a valentine

What I did not say the other day to you for today
Is not unsaid because lost today with such thoughts
    in my head
That make one who looks up at the time say it has
    gone ahead.

36
    Strange
To reach that age,
        remember
  a tide
And full
  for a time
      be young.

37

The world autumn
Spiked seeds on undried branches
The tufted clouds
Where you look
So many falls for you
In the river
And where earth gives
Under each shoe

Past slate rock
You will see what soft blue is
With the sea
Such eyes as you have

38

Belly Locks Shnooks Oakie
When he awoke, he
Scared all the spooks. He
Was some oak, he
       Was.

39

One friend,
Red sealing wax, can say of us,
Their house—a woman and a man
Ate food and talked
Prolonged it but

To write, to sing:

White wax, dear face, Love,
Carry my child,—
Taper,—
Point us like any
Two plants.

40

Celia's birthday poem

No ache, love, 's the way to start the New Year,—
chant, then, "New Year" like "No ache" in your ear,
all the while I praise wind and love your face
above snow that melts over trees' space:
carol "No ache" like "New Year" between trees
that removed still share a few centuries.

41

After Charles Sedley

Not, Celia, that I look for rest
    In what I do or am;
In its own time this song addressed
    To you is not for them:

The hurrying world, our hastes have
    No part in you like me;
Faces stop showing what they crave
    In my attempt to see.

"All that in woman is adored"
    Grows my phrase, and your mind
Sings some hundreds of years to afford
    My cadence in kind.

And if your ears hear me I store
    It in our book *Anew*
Where we last who make Sedley—more
    Than he was perhaps—true.

42

You three:—my wife,
>   And the one, whom like Dante,
>   I call the chief of my friends,

And the one who still writes to me—
>   This morning we are in the mess of history,
>   That low crime, and like the devil in the book of *Job*

Having come back from going to and fro in the earth
>   I will give the world all my hushed sources
>   In this poem, (maybe the world wanted them)

I will be so frank everyone
>   Will be sure I am hiding—a maniac—
>   And no one will speak to me.

In any case, if it happens,
>   I will not regret it one day
>   That I am plain to the simplest.

But you three: my friend, my wife, and you,
>   On whom my face and words weigh
>   For whom pavement becomes too vague

To walk on because of me
>   For whom the cracks in our plastered walls
>   Cry out for me "I die! die!"

So that you want to shut your ears,
>   Who begin to judge that something like my stars
>   Weep on us the falls of black luck,

Who must be like myself and not pity me
>   (I am, after all, of the people whose wisdom
>   May die with them)

Who on top of the years cannot stand the thought
    That my tears too can be wet—
    I will ape a dead poet for you

And tell you of the little spirits of sight
    And the eyes, the beginning of love,
    And of the mouth which is its goal,

And of the appetite, he called heart
    And the reason, 'I call soul'.
    These words are better than I

And if I do die before you, as I have always
        wished,—
    Why, that's nothing new, I have always wished
        it,—
    They may speak to you, the equal

Of your own great anxiety
    As when I should have slept
    This morning and you were awake:

"He walks into door-jambs
    Never sees
    Where he goes

"He must do so many things
    In the morning, shower, brush,
    Clean his glasses a half dozen times,

"Pare his toe nails and cut his toes
    Remove the dirt from his finger nails
    After washing (for a clean person!)

"Shave with a dull blade, bolt breakfast,
    That after all night
    Reaching for his pocket flashlight,

"The kind they use in this war,
    To light up the face of his wrist watch
    'two-thirty'—after going

"To bed at two—
       'Two-fifteen'!
       'Three-fifteen, four o'clock,

" 'It is almost time to get up
       I haven't slept, I don't
       Think I will'—out loud!"

"Please"—"Okay! poet
       Did you ever get up
       Without aching

Without looking grouchy?
       You're not like your old father,
       Everyone looking at you would rather suffer instead of you."

I was thinking, shaving at the mirror,
       Will she write the music I cannot,
       Will he paint, probe, what I cannot

Will the other say the words that escape me?
       Will I, who must, write of my world's battle
       In which I have asked, and which I am not allowed,

To fight? Let your words be my testament.
       For I cannot believe we will not grow from them,
       When not needing even to conceive an aversion for anything

Despite the sage I will be dead
       And my thought in you for yet a while
       Wrapped in your words with a question—

Like that of Job's scourge—
       Do you know you are warmed in the earth
       By the south wind?

A beam of light, then, that you may still question.
       You three not divided, nor from me,
       In silence.

43

To my baby Paul

(After Guido)

Since we can't go back to Tuscany, Dinty,
We'll drink to you and Celia and to Jerry
And place her there who has never seen a
                vineyard—
Drinking Chianti with us for the days
                  when you will be growing.

1

"che di lor suona su nella tua vita"
Continuing with Dante (limbo, THE INFERNO, IV, 77)

The comma in line 1 of this poem is meant as a pause in the expectancy of the dream. Perhaps the capital B of "Break," after the opening quotes of line 2, gives the feeling of some unexpected person taking part in one's expected activity: I was aware in the dream that I was writing a poem and also aware of verses by others.

The word "bay" is what I could reconstruct later from the feeling of the action in the dream, as I moved from place to place, and should convey something of all the meanings of the word "bay": red-brown, the laurel, the laurel wreath, a bay horse, a deep bark or cry, a window-bay, a large space in a barn for storage as of hay or fodder, the state of being kept at a standstill, but more specifically two meanings that seemed to include all the others, they are, an arm of the sea and a recess of low land between hills.

The "glasses of preserves" were sealed with white wax.

The waters teemed like flood waters, but perhaps this is an afterthought. They were certainly *falls*, tons of them off the side, on a curve, and nearly on the level of the ramp, and the ramp seemed to be running away at the curve.

When I awoke the exact words of the poem I dreamt were lost, but those I wrote down still seemed to follow on the events of the dream. Later, that morning, Dante's "which sounds of them, up in that life of thine" seemed an appropriate explanation.

29

"Glad they were there"

. . . e quelle anime liete
si fero spere sopra fissi poli,
fiammando forte a guisa di comete

cosi quelle carole differente-
mente danzando, della sua ricchezza
mi si facean stimar, veloci e lente.

PARADISO, XXIV, 10–12, 16–18.

. . . it is a contradiction to say that a body is continually falling towards another and is at the same time continually flying away from it. The ellipse is a trajectory which, while allowing this contradiction to subsist, at the same time solves it.

. . . the bodily substance of the gold counts only as the embodiment of value . . . In its reality, therefore, it is exchange-value. Its use-value manifests itself solely in the ideal form, in the series of expressions of relative value, in which it enters into relation with the contraposing commodities as the complex of its real use forms. These antagonistic forms of commodities are the real forms in which the process of their exchange has its movement and its being.

DAS KAPITAL, Metamorphosis of Commodities

. . . general theory of electromagnetic field, and in which we constantly have in view the state of matter or the medium by which the field is occupied. While speaking of this state, I must immediately call your attention to the curious fact that, although we never lose sight of it, we need by no means go far in attempting to form an image of it and, in fact, we cannot say much about it.

. . . The second assumption relates to a magnetic field. Without thinking of those hidden rotations of which I have just spoken, we can define this by the so called *magnetic force*, i.e. the force acting on a pole of unit strength.

. . . It is not the motion of a single electron, nor the field produced by it, that can make itself felt in our experiments, in which we are always concerned with immense numbers of particles; only the resultant effects produced by them are perceptible to our senses.

Henrik Anton Lorentz
THEORY OF ELECTRONS, pp. 1, 2, 133

. . . luce e sta verde
Guido Cavalcanti, MADRIGALE

Barely and widely

Barely
    and
        widely

love

they say—
    in these words—

of Paul
    "barely
        twelve"

and of me
    "widely
        published

    throughout
        a long
            career"

So unknown

Celia
    you are the peer-
        ess of this
           song

making the news notes
sing
    as there

our music is called—
    smiling
        "Make sure

call your next book—
        Barely and
                widely"

dear.

1

This is after all vacation. All that
matters is, all that matters—neither am
I, intent on poems, desirous of hearing
all these violin and piano sonatas
every morning for over two weeks and—
tired you would rather not—
as for the young violinist who'ld gallivant
rather than work fingers for stops,
fingers for keys—
yet really not. He will say: *all that* matters.
The music comes from another time
and sings it is *so,*
by it *may we* be believed,
know fingers for keeps,
creditably conceive the changes of times
retained in different pieces of music
as a *matter* of us so *they* are believed:
Beethoven's second and fifth violin and piano
sonatas have come to the measure
of two different rooms,
two instruments affecting a third creature
so young he exists in all rooms;
from low string sounds hautboys, such
as treasure today mere oboes, and now
hunting horns, and again strings are themselves
or flutes in the higher positions,
and from piano keys,
which some fiddlers scorn,
cellos, and from
the G string—airs, airs.
All who matter have come
without effacing *ever,*

so easily said, as unlacing
what is
from what was
those who have just got up
may lead or be led back to bed
having contemplated without template to
flower so.

2

You who were made for this music
or how else does it say you,
move thru your fingers, or your bow arm, lead
to this glory: God has—God's—
but one's deepest conviction—
your art, its use—you, happy,
by rote, by heart. Is thought?
What was broken was sense
but is happy again almost seen,
the first trembling of a string a worth
whose immortal ground drops so often
you plait viable strands for your use.
Or so pride loving itself looks
to more fortunate glory, with a power
apart from the trembling sense
only glory restores.

3

The green leaf that will outlast the winter
       because sheltered in the open:
the wall, transverse, and diagonal ribs
       of the privet that pocket air
              around the leaf inside them
       and cover but with walls of wind:
it happens wind colors like glass shelter,
              as the light's aire from a vault
       which has a knob of sun.

4

A Valentine

This
is
not
more
snow
to
fall

but
a
gust
of
the
softest—
bending

down
the
wood
of
gardens'
branches
into

a
girls
and
boys
pastoral,
old

years
not
to
wink

looks,
middle

life
to
chase,
it's
musical

5

The heights

The sun's white in the high fog
that a thin mist at the eyes
shows to this harbor makes see white
and extends white with wide gray of
water as into some foreign public square—
one yacht sail, few dark screws of smoke
float a deceptively unflowing threshold
for the grayed walls on the other
shore: then like quick speech the pearled cartoon
of skyline, of windows curiously
close to pavement here, what is heights
very near under at this stage.

6

Send regards to Ida the bitch
whose hate's unforgiving,
why not send regards?
There are trees' roots, branchtops
    —as is
one who can take his own life
    and be quit
except he might hurt—as
    he imagines
here he's gone—
a person, two; if not the sun.

7

Stratford-on-Avon

1957

The Midlands' *a* is mostly an *i*
Said like *eye*—
"We don't fancy Shixespeare here—
People come from all over the world
To see the birthplace and the grave—
But we have a picture house we go to;
The top of the station is the way
     to Anne Hathaway's cottage at Shottery,
Mary Arden's house is at Wilmcote, 4 miles
     from Henley Street."
"You've a factory here,
Stratford's become industrial?"
"Not really, those are our gas works
     you see at the bottom."
"You need gas to cook with at that, don't
     you?"
And his remains that two Americans
     and their growing son came to see
Might be thought loving
Those works too—
Tho not so much as the mother
     guiding with her baby in the pram
The three ran across again later,
     several times,
As they strolled thru the town.

She had green eyes—
No tall perch, Helena,
Of the Bard's or Swan's
         midsummer dream,
Rather small Hermia
     with whom tall Helena pleaded,

We, Hermia
Have with our neelds created both one flower,
Both on one sampler, sitting on one cushion,
Both warbling of one song, both in one key—
            we grew together,
        a double cherry, seeming parted.
Not tall personage, rather
Hermia—who as
The course of true love never did run smooth,
Guessed love's hell is
O hell! to choose love by another's eye,
Taught *trial patience*
            a customary cross

            Until
            Theseus judged:
No doubt they rose up early to observe
            the rite of May
Good morrow, friends. Saint Valentine is past:
Begin those wood-birds but to couple now?

Maybe as do all the flowers Shakespeare
            remembered
Today planted in the garden
Back of the Birthplace

Good friend for Jesus sake forbeare
The slab might be thought to pray
            for itself
Stone in the chancel stone
Looked on by the full-blown polychrome
            bust
Which such as it is might also not seem
To fancy Shakespeare here—

Anne Hathaway's burden—

And the new Queen's,
She dedicated
A rose tree
Altogether
Too wiry to see;

123

Or the dark
Young man's
With the Midland *ai*
Forelock,
And a girl on his arm,
Teasing:

"The one blotch
On the Shakespeare arms
In Stratford
Is the Memorial Theatre
A woman planned"
As the family of three
Can no longer
Live by thinking
Has one smile,
"That may not be bad
If it turns out well."

8

This year
that Valentine is
late—

not that the
view
distracts,

on Washington's Birthday
the cold
is

lonely
the Flag too
over Governors Island

between the Statue
of Liberty
and

the cruiser
still
in midwater between

the copings of
two
buildings (as

an island in
itself
towards

the hills of
Staten
Island)

since
Valentine's Day—anchored
for the

Picture Post Card
of the crescent
of

his evening
and the red sky
and

the blue
and
for this once

forever,
the
white

star
that is
you.

9

Ashtray

The baited
bear
on
the ashtray

shows more
flare
than the
tramp

in his whip
tho
perhaps
enough's

there
to
give them
heart.

10

Another Ashtray

Three
crimson
mongrels
bait

the whip
in a boot
on a
leg.

bones,
    Eyzies.

The birds of
    Périgueux
sing back Gaul
    Roman and Jew

Middle Ages slum
    merde at St. Front
pendentive
    of Istanbul

Arcades, basilicas,
    chevets, the Tower
of Vésone
    in honesty

Warning
    Stay away
the wall
    crumbles—

The
    park's
a garden
    landscaped with

A butterfly
    of flowers'
hanging spread
    on ground,

Red rose fall
    in the small
arena's ruin
    red briar

Song in
    marbles of
Bertran de Born
    and Girault de Borneil.

11
Head Lines

A San Francisco chronicle.
The voice of the West.

Paternity: 2 men say
They want boy.

'I'm the father,'
Both men say.

Krushchev
won't debate
satellites.

12
4 Other Countries

Merry, La Belle
    antichi, tilling—
of pastime and
    good company:

Tea in England
    as much as you eat
it saves face
    the fill hole's petite—

Luggage, the
    tour complete
the buttocks
    wet—

On the way to
    Tours, the russet

cow, bordering
the river

La Gloire in the black
flags of the valley
of the
Loire——

A lavender plough
in Windermere
the French blue
door

Of a gray
stone
house in
Angers

Walled farms
little lanes
of entry, orange-
red roofs

A period farm
cowboy on
a live green
rivulet

Longs
for ranches
cultivated
plains

A horse opera
of Indians
to end with
the train's past.

On the route
to Poitiers
a garden of
purple and red

As only the French
can plant
in front of
an arcade of poplars'

Arc de triomphe
infusing all
madeleine memories
of the Ouest.

Bedlam
Paris
Roman
London——

Where stop
who have spoken to
old friends
for the

First time
years
sing to
speak

There is no
quiet in the
world——a
wedding-

Cake Tower of
Babel
that is
Nice——

Nor drive
chasing
shape
in rock

Color
of Lascaux

This hush that
    the bard
is writing
    again

The vowels
    abide
in consonants
    like

Souls
    in
bodies—
    paradise is his

Hand,
    paradise
our
    speech;

To perfect
    makes
practice,
    a ray of

Sun
    he spoke
too soon,
    as on the

Legendary
    map
the
    criminal

Dropping
    always in
monk's garb
    into the

Grot
    lower

than the
    rise

He
    first
began,
    as a hole

In a head
    St. Michael
made
    in a bishop

Sent
    to sit
for an
    eternity

To look thru
    one window
of a
    Merveille

Not with eyes
    but after
he had died
    and built

Up to the mount
    where the Druids
in white surplice
    sacrificed—

Red drops
    blinking
to the Three Kings
    rubies—

Master
    Aristotle's eternal
whiteness of
    a day.

Benedictine
    initial—
golden green
    serving

Pontorson
    with croissant
on breakfast
    gingham

A
    bottle of
liqueur
    Michelaine

A tourist
    forgot in
the gap
    of a removed stone

Under an
    arch of
a
    stairway

Of the
    Perilous
Castle,
    under

Which
    endless wind
stirring
    reflections

Of clouds
    reaches water
on an Elysium
    of sand—

Yellow,
    pearl,

shadow,
    gloss-

Black—
    in one's
youth
    old women

Begged in
    the street
all the way to
    the archangel

Saint Cecelia
    who cannot praise
them
    smiles

They have
    turned young
again in shops
    on sales

Of fake
    Quimper,
Durham's
    more solid

With Bede's tomb,
    Chartres'
two towers
    as once

Measure
    Leoninus
to
    Josquin.

Merry
    La Belle are
England
    France

Short of
    a month
of pastime
    blossoms

The wish
    that of
good company
    there be

No end
    sped around
wall
    of rock

Over
    the Middle
Sea
    to where—

He
    was at
via Marsala 12
    an era gone

Now known
    of no one
except Gino Pasterino
    an old man

Assures from
    that balcony
we looked
    down.

The noise the
    beach of parasols
obscures—
    the place

Gets no rest
    from the sea

it hides now
   —nor eyes.

Understanding:
   I wasn't going to say
for fear
   You didn't want to hear.

That's the worst
   of understanding,
a handshake
   would be better.

And of
   Antichi
there is
   no end.

That song
   is the kiss
it keeps
   is it

The
   unsaid worry
for what
   should last.

By the intimacy
   of eyes,
or its inverse—
   restiveness

Of heart—
   Pisa's Baptistry,
Nicollà Pisano's
   pulpit

Cannot—*antichi*—
   hold a candle
to light the
   circle of rock

Sculptures
    in the shadow
of round
    wall—

Primitive
    monumental
nameless
    as the carver

Who hewed—
    constraining
his shapes
    to rocks,

A lion and Judah
    perhaps,
a king—David
    by his harp,

The mother—
    married to
his line—
    her granite

Suckling
    the child—
manifest
    as the thigh

Of the
    Triumphant God
on the mosaic
    Judgment

Seat
    that Cimabue
directed
    in the semidome

Over the apse
    of the Cathedral

across
        the close.

Beside this
        seen that
legs
        would walk to

Duccio's
        chromatic story
in Siena's
        museum

Is subtle
        only
when lighting
        from

The green hills
        and knolls
the great and
        true candle

That lifts
        his countryside
which it lights
        today,

As, again, out
        of all
profluent
        Florence

A great cow
        of rock
on
        a plinth

In the Museo
        Opera del Duomo
is,
        first, valid,

More than any
	later takes
of Giotto
	in paint

And should be
	after the
stillborn
	recent ruin, a

Chapel
	in Santa Croce
selling gilt
	red leather bags.

Fra Angelico's brother
	painted one stiff
crucifixion
	after another

One
	in each
cell
	down one

Of two rows
	on the
top floor of
	San Marco

Each
	martyr's wall
his
	torture,

His
	angelic
brother
	who kneeled and rose

For the opposite row
	of cells

breathed the
    whole Legend:

A horse
    or a baby
two crossed trees
    or a mother,

In one fresco
    the luminous
center
    a piece of bread

The Lord of His
    own Last Supper
holds to the mouth
    of its inseparable Guest,

All who eat there
    inseparable.
For one afternoon
    looking down

From San Miniato
    on the flower
structure across
    the Arno

We may miss
    the Masaccio's
no distance below
    in the Carmine,

But
    if they are
for all time
    there will

Be another time,
    as in Rome
after
    the rising abstract

Of square
      futurist
coliseum,
      the Fall

Before
      the Decline
built a
      ruin to order

And Nobody's
      priority
of holes
      to come.

After
      Church
rose on
      the Forum

And this
      dug up,
churches
      fell

They square
      the marble
faced
      oval

And after
      Henry
qualmishly
      shy

Of Chaim
      (life)
and an Adams
      he read

Himself
      Adam

(earth)
        "—Why!

Why! !
        Why! ! !—"
Because
        his blood

Chilled,
        for whom
a Jew
        and friend

Is embarrassed—
        there is
other time
        repeating

Like his neighbor
        the blind beggar
on the steps
        of Ara Coeli

Altar of Heaven
        cypresses hide stars
candles shine towards
        cypresses

The column of
        Trajan so
small
        below

The grandeur is brutal
        only in the cast
in the Victoria
        & Albert.

Rome is a low
        city of shuttered houses
with
        tawny or orange views

142

Its older ruins
        so gentle
they disappear,
        to have been

Like the old brick
        Roman wall
that falls lower than
        any new apartment,

And the Pantheon's dome
        if stripped of its coffers
is but the adolescence
        of a geometry

That pours steel concrete.
        Familial, travelled,
or effeminate,
        the Romans loved

To possess and please
        not size so much as small
marbles of Greek gods,
        and also their wives

Daughters and sons: unlike
        the Christians
in the catacombs
        who burying theirs

In their walls
        must have turned
in distraction
        to give joy

To one another
        in carving
good shepherds
        and their flocks

Or painting fish
        or ravens

when their hymns
　　and prayers

Brought no daily
　　bread—and for fear no
other speech than
　　out of their wild eyes.

Tendril vine
　　stem
grape
　　bud

Leaf flower
　　the Roman work's
gentlest in
　　the baths of Diocletian,

Stone skirts
　　stone girl
drapes them on her
　　wet and wind blown.

Farnesina
　　stuccoes are
a snow's conceiving
　　of white,

Four
　　walls
of a room
　　restoring Livia's

Villa Ad Gallinas
　　carry continuous
garden, the green
　　singing with birds

Where fruits shine orange.
　　Stele
grow,
　　mosiac

Tesserae
 animal and
abstract, each
 is animate.

In germ
 the ribbed vault
on a sarcophagus,
 also a tiny

Fan vault—
 so proportioned
as not to excite
 later doubts of lavishness.

So the unribbed
 vault at
San Vitale
 hints at the rib

But remains
 where
the eye can take in
 gold, green and blue:

The gold that shines
 in the dark
of Galla Placidia,
 the gold in the

Round vault rug of stone
 that shows its
pattern as well as the stars
 my love might want on her floor

The quiet better than crying
 peacock is immortal
she loves, knows
 it so pretty

That pretty in
 itself is enough

to love.
    She likes:

The Bell Tower
    in Venice
whose windows
    run not down

The center
    but along the side
edge; the three
    gonfalon

Poles before
    St. Mark's Basilica
like votive candles
    for the five

Kisses of the cusped
    lunettes
of the second
    story;

The bare south wall
    relieved by a tile
as tho it hung
    upon a wall at home.

Nothing is
    even,
so
    touches.

She
    came to Venice
by night
    a love that fears

Water
    and trusts the
stranger balance
    of the gondolier,

146

It is not a question
    with the red purple gold
of houses in water
    of a torture

Making paint stone
    or stone
wrongly
    flesh.

The Banda Municipale
    plays Boccherini's
"Menuetto"
    in the lit

Shadow of the night
    sky the roof of
the public reception hall
    of the Piazza

Ledges of
    whose palaces and church
crowd
    the pigeons asleep.

Bright to the morning
    they feed
on the swell
    of the Grand Canal

Who can drive past
    the new church of
Jesu Lavoratore,
    poor carpenter.

The faded
    fresco
in San Zeno
    of Verona,

Of the mourning
    of Jesus

down
      from the cross—

Eyes
      cannot tell
if leaves
      cover the weeping

Or if the mottles
      shred colors
where plaster flaked,
      never meant

For leaves,
      the statue
of San Zeno
      himself looks Buddhist,

And the Han-
      like carving
of the small sculptured
      squares of the bronze

Doors of San Zeno
      come much nearer
Heaven than
      Ghiberti's gates.

Of good company
      then
the screed
      is:

To Montecchio
      to eat well
for two houses
      'star-cross'd'

Or history is
      so
as the wrinkled
      signora in black

Head shawl
    says kindly
'the young from
    everywhere, as far as

America,
    come here for
Giulietta's Tomb'
    stand at

The broken lid
    (it might be
a bath)
    of the marble coffin,

A coil of
    climbing plant
comes down
    thru the grate

In the ground
    of the overhead cloister
to look
    also;

That Sunday is
    best to eat a
fruit and not
    cross the Adige

For the Roman theatre
    we see across it,
and not go
    to sit in the

Box
    of the Gens Valeria
where—a question if—
    Catullus sat?

Sirmio, almost the
    eye of islands

o Lydiae lacus
    Garda, gem,

Mine;
    this is it
which makes it
    worth it;

Three months go;
    that the innocent
pyramid of red and blue
    that suffers at the eating

Is for the movement
    of the hands to it
and the mind
    that willed **to eyes;**

One work of art
    to a room, the exhibit in
Milano's Sforzesco
    shows is enough;

The fresco
    or tempera
is, as of Luini,
    of green and wheat;

As on the other
    side of the Alps
the peasants
    meet Parliament;

Quiet;
    tilling;
the uplifted frozen
    wave of Pilatus;

A man
    tilling
mountain
    upland;

Liveable
    place;
whose character is
    endurable

As the eyes are moist before
    the regularly spaced
flower window boxes
    of Berne; the

Aare
    flows below, above the
old city
    old or new there's

No
    architecture
to speak of;
    walk.

Of travel's
    sickness
one's young son
    puns

Guiltless
    if world-
bred,
    'The reason

I threw up
    was not a Confucian egg
nor a Lao-tse but
    a bad egg.

How's *your* Duomo?'
    Returned to the sea
past point of no
    return

Leans over
    the deck rail—

'Not worth
        being sick for'—

It blows up
        its furtive hush
a sound that
        loses sound in

Blued white:
        'Lace.' Laundry.
'But'
        he says

'Can you
        describe it—
always
        different.'

Practice
        in lifeboat drill.
A baby in blue
        storm cape's

First to be wheeled
        off the gangplank,
the tug with something
        like a fig leaf approaches

The ship's bow.
        Go home.
There you may
        think of it.

The pyramid
        repeats
of the peaks.
        Colorado's *Red Rocks:*

The natural
        acoustics
of the amphitheatre
        between the two

Sandstone shapes
　　they call
Creation
　　and *Shipwreck*.

As the eyes
　　near wreck
to create
　　when they see

RAIL　　CROS (S)
SING　　ROAD
of pastime
　　and good company.

Index of First Lines and Titles *

* Titles in capitals